impossible bottle

SOUTHERN MESSENGER POETS

Dave Smith, Series Editor

impossible bottle

poems

CLAUDIA EMERSON

Louisiana State University Press Baton Rouge

Published by Louisiana State University Press
Copyright © 2015 by Claudia Emerson
All rights reserved
Manufactured in the United States of America
First printing

Designer: Barbara Neely Bourgoyne
Typeface: Whitman
Printer and binder: Thomson-Shore, Inc.

The author thanks the following publications where these poems first appeared. *Academy of American Poets:* "Fast"; *Atlanta Review:* "My Mother Senses Them" and "Westerns"; *The Australian Journal of Medicine:* "The Anatomy Lesson: Resection"; *The Missouri Review:* "Infusion Suite": 1, 2, 3 4, 6, and 9; *One:* "MRI"; *Poetry:* "Metastasis: Worry-Moth"; *Subtropics:* "Cyst" and "Pasture Accident"; *TAB (Tabula Poetica):* "Last the Night."

For their support and advice during the writing of this book, I would like to thank Kent Ippolito, Catherine MacDonald, Leslie Shiel, Betty Adcock, Rod Smith, Debra Nystrom, Lisa Russ Spaar, MaryKatherine Callaway, Dave Smith, my Sewanee colleagues, my students in the spring 2014 graduate workshop at VCU for the inspiration of their discipline, and the members of Treeshop, you know who you are.

Library of Congress Cataloging-in-Publication Data
Emerson, Claudia, 1957–2014
  [Poems. Selections]
  Impossible bottle : poems / Claudia Emerson.
    pages ; cm. — (Southern messenger poets)
  ISBN 978-0-8071-6082-4 (cloth : alk. paper) — ISBN 978-0-8071-6083-1 (paperback : alk. paper) — ISBN 978-0-8071-6084-8 (pdf) — ISBN 978-0-8071-6085-5 (epub) — ISBN 978-0-8071-6086-2 (mobi)
  I. Title.
  PS3551.N4155A6 2016
  811'.54—dc23

                                                                2015000308

for Kent, always,

and

for my physicians:

Dr. Brian Jay Kaplan
Dr. Leopoldo Fernandez
Dr. Steven Grossman
Dr. Andrew Poklepovic
Dr. Elisabeth Weiss
Dr. William Broaduss

And for the medical students, interns, and staff at
VCU's Massey Cancer Center—
and for my colleagues and fellow writers at
Virginia Commonwealth University.

> This World is not Conclusion.
>
> —EMILY DICKINSON

She doesn't put great emphasis on death.

> He gathered the waters of the sea as in a bottle;
> he put the deeps in storehouses.
>
> —PSALM 33:7

grounded in faith

downplays death, seems to have Biblical references

CONTENTS

anatomies

infusion suite

participant observations

impossible bottle

impossible bottle

anatomies

Metastasis: Intercession

[too late   here   perhaps   for some
intercession]   the physician

speaks to his screen   instead   to the all
of you it has

become   his words not imagined
now   but real   and

your   sorrow is ecstatic   something
you do not feel

you hear your own voice   at a distance
in the abelia bush

outside   at home   [a voiceless   God]
flames   there   late bees

a burn   slow   miraculous such green   there
there you are

Choppy, like a heartbeat

3

MRI

At rest, the machine makes a softer sound,
almost pleasant, something

like a lone cricket, perfected in its measure.
But the technician is too

bright, illuminant as the room—talking
with someone in the glassed

control booth about Dixie Donuts—and so
overweight I cannot

imagine she could fit herself into the tube
where she will send me

in minutes It is Friday, late afternoon;
there can't be many of us

left to see She feeds me into the mouth
of the thing, telling me

to follow the breathing directions as best I can,
and I do, for the next

three quarters of an hour, breathe in and out
and pray, curse, clench my teeth,

sorry as I have ever been for myself   *self pity & self-awareness
and suddenly sorrier   all at once*

to realize that I am the last of the many
this day; someone else's

face was just this close to the low ceiling,
someone else's worry

saw this flat whiteness. In my hand I hold
the small, bulbous call

button everyone must hold, with the same
nervous lightness, I can

imagine holding a moth—so as not to kill it
and not to let it go.

The metaphor for it metastasizes, too:
I am in the belly

of the beast, the belly of a whale, in some sterile
wilderness, desert

island, sand-blind; I am a thread in the deep
eye of a needle; in some

percussive otherworld that rises up
every time I exhale

and hold still my empty lungs. And then I come to
and settle on a tunnel,

a real one, the one they call the Paw Paw
for the nearby trees,

and a day in early June three years ago,
and I can stay in there

long enough to survive it again—artifact
of a place, a quarter mile

through a mountain in western Maryland.
You are never out

of sight of the end of it, and still you find
you do need that borrowed

flashlight you thought you could do without, its battery
feeble, jittery beam.

Mules and men died in here, hauling out
the stone to make this

passage, narrow towpath alongside a stream
of water you can hear

but cannot see. The way out is searing
and round, a worthless sun

that lights nothing but itself, and still you choose it,
the entrance behind you

just as fixed but changed, somehow, another
state, no, another country,

farther away, now, you are sure, than this.

6

Metastasis: Chevron

there you are   in seeing
first its habit

received form   the old   V
a figment   against

[a February-blank sky]
the bird   [deviant]

albino   the one become
sillouette cut-out

as in   relief   its flight the same
flawless   as the ones

around it   barest blemish
joy in its being   unseen

for a moment   immutable   inside
your brain

Well

When I first knew it, it was already a structure
of sheer sentiment,

more remnant than place, covering the old,
neglected depth it took

to get to water. My mother's uncle—whose voice
I can't recall ever

hearing—built it, the tall wall he knew to sink
there because of sycamores—

ghostly water-seekers—seemingly out
of place, and a well-eye

he must have noticed brimming with ferns. The same
water in the house

would later be made plain by comparison,
tepid, tamed by spigot

and pipe, basin and drain, our chapped hands
always in it, under it.

It is not so hard now to understand what was
for a long time unrecognizable,

a given, that source as absence of something,
a backing out of this—

pipe, house, us—all of this, so perfect
as to be invisible.

Metastasis: Owl

your⌈brain the bewildered margin
of this city⌉

its river   from here   you hear
believe   and cannot

see ⌊you mistake a voice
at dusk for human⌉

or something   ordinary   until
the hour escapes

your ignorance to pass
over   close

enough for you to feel
the air it moves

its sight   poor   majestically
so   as yours

Murder Ballad

Now and again a car drives by it slowing,
curious, the kind

of tourist I hate and have been of late, new here,
jogging the neighborhood,

block after block of strange doors, closed stories.
Imagining narratives

worse than my own has become a kind of balm—
but all of them are kept

secreted as this can never be—
and so I circle it

again and again: A New Year's day, weather
indecisive as March,

doors left unlocked, this one ajar; adrift
on the porch the smell of cooking.

Whatever might have been overheard, no one
did hear, or could recall

apart from the ordinary shrieks of children winter-
crazed, or a crowd's televised

screaming in someone else's living room;
no one had the capacity

to imagine otherwise, the house
an ordinary brick

foursquare on its corner, awningless,
shutterless, a countenance

folks thought incapable of such imposture.
Bound, muzzled, bludgeoned,

that whole of that family was set to burn.
The smoke was what

the people saw. I am here a decade after
the mourning flowers,

the yellow-ribboned lot, the gawkers. Some other
family dares to live in it

now; other children's things clutter the porch.
But the space must recall it,

the rooms, the air—no widow left to do it,
no orphan. Surely, place

cannot be parted from this—the absolute
nothing worse of it—

though every single morning the tree before it
shades and sways,

and smoke rises from the chimney, the way it does
from the one next door,

the way it does from my own, neglected for it;
the roof sheds rain.

Metastasis: Worry-Moth

yours is not the majestic   Gypsy
the Codling   Luna   Wax   or grander

Atlas   with the appetite
of a plague   entire fields

succumbing to them   whole
generations of bees   this is

the unseen   closeted   unassuming
gray that seeks out last winter's

cloth   another season   drawn
to the body's scent   what was

its heat   to consume early   that scant
much of you   fragile   lace-like

the constellate   erasures   of the coat
it makes for you to wear

*medical coat? Comparing doctor
to a moth or vice versa*

Chain Chain Chain

Thirty years to the day since the virgin-time:
a nephew was the ring-

bearer, the rings tied down with slick ribbons
to the small satin pillow

on which he bore them. Pretending to pray, I watched
ants crawl across his shined shoes.

The pastor who declared it is long dead from cancer.
My brother as well;

that morning he came stoned, his hair long,
aviator sunglasses

blinding mirrors; and the brother-in-law and the in-laws,
my own father, all dead.

The friend who would later put a pillow over
her face and shoot herself

through it, knew what I wanted, and sent it wrapped
in butcher paper:

a Mexican wedding dress, white on white
embroidery, stitches dense,

intricate—the seamstress's signature a single
black strand of her hair

sewed into the yoke. It was, indeed, perfect.
It is. The April air is

chill as it has ever been. I dance to *chain*
chain chain before I take it

off again and feed it to the fire I have set
for this. There was

a garden, a watchful gardener, a small
cement pool, fat carp, a statue

of a little girl carved into her dress of stone,
her face abstracted by moss.

Metastasis: English Ivy

it makes for these   winter
trees to wear

green-thick stockings   a blight
of sleeves   the English

ivy thriving   in[neglect]
the ones dead]   who

thought to teach it   to love
their gates   pergolas   their

brains   to see [the pretty
limits they thought

they could make]   for you   inheriting
instead   the escaped

these trees   full and green
with [their mistake]

*to love is to be
neglected, disappointed, to
limit other*

*interior failing, growth
as death?*

*are there all derived from the same
metastasized metaphor? Do all they all have
to do w/ metastasis?*

Weather

for Kent

They said they had no category for it,
a hybrid thing they christened

and numbered anyway. The meteorologists
couldn't help but be

delirious; its center massive and slow,
its ocean-born body

coming inland then as bodies, one winter,
one tropical, a conjoined

thing no one had ever seen; how healthy
it was, they marveled, how

determined—part cyclone, blizzard, part hurricane,
tornado, all of it,

all of it applied. They pointed to maps,
measurements and charts;

they struggled to track it, predict what it
might do. Already numberless

outages, closures. Here—you had catalogued,
stored up what we might need—

batteries, candles, canned fruit, bottled water,
matches, the transistor

radio. We listened to the wind;
we waited. You were more

restless than I was, going out again
and again onto the porch,

to see for yourself, leaning into it,
almost as though to dare it,

test it, touch the hem of it, or let it
touch you; before you knew,

you knew it would spare us.

Metastasis: Web

no mistake   this web's expanse
near invisible

in cornered light   the screened porch-door
open year round   the world's

entrance to it   the wren's
discovery   the accident

the web become larder   the spider
grocer   its lovely apron

filament   parcels of the air
asleep   and bound   [and you

*spiders, often evil +
gross, here are merchants
of a kinder, quicker version
of death than the one
she is living*

approve   somehow of the commerce]
as though   agreed to

to God   the ease of deft return   [the joy
such   swift   excision]

longing for a quick death

18

Ornithography: Preparing the Study Skin

People know to call him when they find one—
a heron collapsed on the bank

of the canal, a cardinal having mistaken
glass for air, the dove

I found in our garden. He keeps them all in a freezer
in the lab, bagged in plastic,

a random, patient flock—until he finds
an hour on a weekend afternoon,

a Sunday like this one the quietest, the science building
empty, lab serene

beneath the hum of florescence. The process
is the same no matter the bird,

though a starling has the toughest flesh, he says,
and a mourning dove like mine

the thinnest, like tissue paper. He lays out the implements,
simple and few, tweezers,

scalpel, scissors, some thread: First, he places cotton down
the throat to absorb the blood.

After breaking the humerus bone, he loosens the wings
from the body, makes a simple

incision, then, straight down the belly to peel back
skin from the muscles

encasing organs, turns the body inside out.
He scoops the brain, the way

he might a yolk from an egg—scoops out the eyes,
surprisingly large, given

the size of the skull. He wants me to see how it is
translucent as porcelain,

holds it up to show me how the light
passes through. The body

mass, the brain, the eyes he replaces with cotton.
The wings he secures

to the sides of the body, finishing by fixing
crossed feet and bill neatly

with sewing thread, then binding the whole to a stick
like something about to be

burned alive. It is, after all, not meant
to remind but to instruct,

he says—so that we are allowed to see what was
kept from us, the color phases

of the screech owl, the very fringe that soundproofed
deadliest flight, here, touch it—

all of it prepared, collected, labeled, and kept
for this in narrow drawers—

part catalogue, part library, part still-formed twin
of the garden where I found it.

Metastasis: Tree House

small room excised   from air
a ladder lashed to it

you don't trust as much as   the air
you do   there is

a basket   a pulley and rope   an armless
rocking chair   the trunk

risen through the floor with a chimney's
green pretense   of heat

[you are a child's afternoon
without the child]   who

was not meant   either   to stay here
and so you stay

[you are that same   thoughtless-
ness] [no   afterthought]

↓

no point, just existing
OR
an afterthought to the world

Blood-Groove

My brother was angry; I understand that
now, the Boy Scouts my mother

led all trying to build fires inside circles
she had taught them to make

of stone. With no choice but to bring me with her,
she left me alone

to gather my own rocks and tinder; I recall
dry grass and twigs, skeletal

leaves, the small cardboard drawer with the one
wooden match I was

allowed, the rasp of the strike, my fire the first
to blaze and with such brightness

I could not help but call out from it—to my mother,
to all the boys. He drew

his knife, held it by the tip, then threw it
for all he was worth,

shaft and blade, blood-groove, and bone handle, sailing
end over end, until

it found the outer orbit of my left eye,
where I will always be

able to measure the size of its strike, the depth
of its impression

that of a grain of rice. I never asked—
and will never know

what were his chances, what was his aim, by
how much he might have

missed his mark, or how close he came.

Metastasis: The James

all afterthought   this late
morning   ⌈it takes

life as death   selfishness

another town's rain   into
itself   for   itself⌉

swells   with its snow   its trash
it supplants its own

banks   the fields   of what

brain failing ⌈your brain must

accept   now   as vision   blank
as sight⌉   widening

the narrowing ⌈you will know
when all of it

*you only are certain of
death   when you die*⌉

recedes⌉   it will
intercede   to see   you   see

The Anatomy Lesson: Resection

You didn't know what to do with the wisdom teeth,
so you saved them for a while,

for nothing, or what to think of the ganglion cyst—
smooth, benign—they removed

from the wrist just above the pulse. And then
there was the first biopsy

of the cervix, a plug the size of a pencil eraser,
they said, and that mole

you'd had all your life they all of a sudden called
suspicious, and the nuisance

the gallbladder became, and the thyroid gland.
But it is the tumor

in the gut that gets everyone's attention,
its slow, mute explosion

in the liver. This time, you are the anatomy
lesson, your surgery

a sharper degree of difficulty. Starched,
bleached, their names newly

stitched on crisp lapels, the medical students
file in and listen;

they write things down. They observe the operation;
there is a quiz, a test;

you are the exam; what they can access of you,
theater—now—in the surround;

you are the text, the close reading and radical
revision, the offensive

part lifted out and taken away in a pan,
fetus-like—brain-like

that kind of measure, that kind of heft. Only
they can tell you, when you

return to them, what you can live without, what
regenerates, and on hearing it,

you feel a lightening, the way a snake must
on slipping through its discarded

mouth into another year, or, knowing nothing
of a year, into time itself.

infusion suite

1

The nurse puts on the protective gown for this one,
sky-blue, crepe paper-like. She asks again
for me to verify name, date of birth,
checking what I say against the information
on the small plastic bag she shows to me
before hanging it upside down, its contents
impossibly clear, benign looking
as water coursing the clearest bore—
umbilical-like, that almost invisible line.
The trees outside the tall window appear
still full with summer, crows' flight—more
like drunken tumbling—something to see
while I agree that *yes, yes, this is me.*

2

The poplars outside this place an old stand,
their trunks rise, slender nudes that sway in a rush
of wind and sun. At the trees' edge, someone
has hung feeders to distract us from ourselves,
and so I don't look at her when she says
to the screen of her computer that my blood
numbers are good, better, in fact, than last

time. Hour after hour, we watch birds circle
the plastic cylinders of sunflower seed,
cling to the caged cakes of suet swinging
from tall hooked poles—not unlike ours, I like
to think, their source of flight gravity-measured,
a given, too—and we are all radiant with it.

3

The surgery was a flash
fire in the yard, folks

nearly delirious
with rakes and hoses, their

faces hot with it.
This place is the slow

burn they watch, if they do,
at a safer distance, as

they might a neighbor's field
smoldering, glad it's

not their own, their concern
now the direction of

the wind, a chance of rain.

4

Leonard, he shrugs the name patch on his shirt;
his cancer back after a good year and a half;
it's worse this time; then tells me just as much

a matter of fact he is a mechanic
at the collision place, his specialty the under

-carriage of a car after a wreck,
realignment, the stuff nobody ever sees
and will never notice unless—no, until—

it gets out of whack; he's lucky, though,
his brother's bone marrow a match, the one
he had not spoken to in thirty years;

he will go into work tomorrow, has to, that new guy—
he shrugs again—some brand new kind of stupid.

5

I am not this, not here, this time. I am
what I mistook for a shadow

in our walled garden, gathered beneath the concrete
bench, concrete also the sky,

like the cold, sorrowful bottom of something; it is
a collared shadow, though—a stray cat

I see us feeding in the afternoon. And I
will watch it eat from a dish

on the back stoop, then bathe in the open doorway
of the garage, in that narrow shaft

of afternoon light, where I will be also,
and also behind it, where I am

the body of light that swings from the rafters.

6

The trees redden beneath it, before loss,
becoming livid with this: rain, cold, windless,
shadowless the light, the sky a low

opalescence. This one a quieter day,
the room empties earlier. I eat
a bowl of soup from the table I make

of my lap. Later, I will win at scrabble,
studying my sorry trough of letters—
CAUSE double its worth, though, and I puzzle it

with UZ—as in Job, as in the land of—triple—
cheating, really, but we agree we will
let it go this time, all my words small

but costly, and my accounting of them perfect.

7

gray on gray this

scale the woman's

face her counts so

low her lips blanched

to this parchment

where I write her

even her eyes

faded paling

to a sameness moth-like

her expression

the sameness shifting

fog that pretends

to know no noon

8

I know the nurses' names by now, recognize
several patients, our familiarity
with each other that of folks on the same bus,
its slowness a shared slow-jolt alarm, the lumbering

maddening, then numbing. A woman I have never
seen, purple-turbaned, prefers jaundiced leaves,
birdless feeders someone forgot to fill
to any of us. I have chosen to look out

that window at what passes for the world.
We all have. What we do not know about
each other can go unspoken; our old ordinary

means nothing here, and we know already
the ordinary that this is—and is—.

9

The old woman next to me does not speak
all day, not even to the young girl who came

to be with her, a granddaughter, perhaps,
with nails painted the same electric blue

she used to paint her grandmother's nails,
and perhaps she was the one who plaited

the single tight gray braid—a pinned, frayed

aura around her head. Her eyes occluded,
clouded over, the older woman appears

to look me in the eye, though, to hold me in
an iron-steady gaze, the cataracts

small blinds she has early drawn down,
defiant, and she stands behind having done it.

10

The Mayan calendar ran out
a week ago, and still

this year ends on what we insist
is an eve, the day

ledge-like, gate-like, a transom.
A man in the waiting

room opens a penknife and begins
to scrape away at what

I have mistaken for his palm—
a lottery ticket,

scratch-and-win, and he is
delirious with it, this

small chance (why not?) all.

11

We have come in from what was earlier
predicted to be ice, the steady pour instead
washing away last scraps of snow. The man
across the way opens his lunch: a block of cheese,
saltines, a jar of sweet pickles. He chooses
from among them thoughtfully; the excess syrup
he lets drip back into the jar before removing
his choice from the blade of his penknife. All this

tires him. When he is finished, he covers his eyes
with his jacket's empty sleeve. I see it is too easy
a metaphor, and though nothing will wake him
all afternoon, I will not mistake his
loosely sleeved sleep for anything else.

12

I bring a tray of puddings
to share on my

last day. Each cup is different,
some topped with berries,

some with peppermints.
I give everyone

a small wooden spoon,
the kind I recall

from elementary school
birthday parties,

something you use once,
throw away,

think nothing of.

participant observations

Pasture Accident

Fog that morning all of them waded.
They were used to her

voice, her hand on their spines, their flanks, her fingers
in their manes, their tails,

the pressure she brought to bear on the bits they let her
slip into their mouths.

Iron the instant, then, when she bent to fasten
a buckle on a blanket—

the physics a wrecking ball's, the hoof's wall
and sole that knew best

this pasture's perimeters now sank that same
kind of deep into her

cheekbone, brow, her nose, forehead, jaw,
the orbit of her eye

crushed and with it that side of the world.
She came to near-blind,

the blood already cool and clotting; through it
she heard grass moving,

the arrhythmia of grazing, a bored sigh.
The fog had lifted to rain;

she could make out a crow drinking from a pocked
hoof-print in the mud—

as though from something breakable—what remained
of a horse, of a pasture.

Mortuary Make-Up Artist

The medicine cabinet has become her, her face
a small door she opens

and closes—its store her closeted cures,
prescriptions for sorrow,

a vial for the self in beauty school, the corpses
she trains for—her body

the wall, wall socket, and drain. Everyday
she wears a smock, wide,

gaping pockets, carries a rigid, plastic
caddy—a neatened arsenal

of tiny scissors, tweezers, a razor, lotions,
and liners for their eyes,

their lips. The penny on the tongue is her idea,
she thinks, a coppery

lozenge not unlike the sadness she savors
to spend and spend like this—

this one, insoluble syllable.

Last the Night

Sickness kept her house the way winter
kept the garden, a betrothal;

what had been forgotten at its outset
remained so—what little

it did recall uneasy, vague, the birdbath's
surface opaque as milk-

glass, the pansies in bright collapse. The mail
collected like leaves wind-

gathered in corners; books she had abandoned
facedown, every one somewhere

near a beginning. But the sundial
remained fluent in light—

in time—and afternoons slowly returned
to her, tempting the window

open wide as though for milder air,
her elbow on the sill,

a cusp, where she learned to trick birds
into mistaking her cupped

hand for the feeder she had hung next to it,
her arm like the thin

column of a candle, and she had perfected
its going away with night,

the way it did not tremble beneath the flame.

A Thought

Somewhere in her brain there is a cognitive
map, a constellation

of place-cells sunk deep in gray matter—and there,
a man, the one she told

no to, refuses to disappear with that
long-ago summer where

she borrowed a house, as though to borrow him,
or time. There, she has

planned it, the farewell pleasant she knows he will
argue against. He likes

even the word *mistress*, the hiss of it,
its gloss a lingering kiss.

She draws a deep tub, lights candles along
the edge, water releasing

steam like guilt, grief, relief. He is behind her
in the bath, saying something,

nothing, his hands warm and wet encircling
not her shoulders now

but her throat with what the brain might not have
stored at all—so close

to ordinary the gesture. He lets them
linger like the thought

he has or does not have, about what he
could but would not do,

one finger tracing the hollow notch that knits
her collarbones together,

for the last time, tracing it. He will sleep well
and rise before her

in the morning. He has brought fresh cherries
in a paper bag; it rustles

with the movement of his hand as he replaces
each one with its pit,

methodical such capable hunger.
He will return to his wife,

his children, the shop where he sells suet
and seed, to the bell

he hung so that it tinkles sweetly when
someone enters, enticed

by the brightly painted houses for bats
and birds. *Come in, Come in,*

it says to them, and again, now, to her,
as he smiles from behind

the counter, just a thought, enjoying how
it does not fail to become him.

Ecology

Bitterness, here, is not a curdling or a preserve;
it is, after so many

years, an ecology, something she cultivates
like the moss that grows

between the stones in the garden; not trusting
its proven love of shade,

she pours buttermilk on it, the acidity
she knows to be pleasing.

How dare this remind her of the great-aunt
who raised her, of the mink

stole she wore to church, precious thing, cage-
raised, bred for the neck.

She recalls the small chain that bound it,
the way it seemed to hold

its rear feet in its teeth, the mirror-shine
of its eyes. The way it saw

her and only her.

Cyst

She had once had an abortion, she said, and later
an affair with a married man,

then another, her solitude always
uneasy, her body

lonely for something nameless as they had been,
or as she made them.

She said it began as pressure not quite pain,
and they found it outside

the womb, clinging to an ovary, having
conceived of itself.

When they removed it, they told her she could see it
if she wanted to:

just a curiosity with teeth, hair, and nails. Odd
but benign, the doctor

said, most always benign, nodding toward it
as though it could agree

with him, as though that were the fact,
the whole of it: curious

mistake a body can make.

Fast

Her daughters were born fast, three in a row,
the older two the ordinary

disappointment most girls are to their fathers,
the third one *God's child,*

she said, declaring it so; *bird-stupid,* he called it,
slow as a log chain

through mud. The house she would never leave
was on the steepest street

in town, and the older girls learned there to be fast
on skates and sleds, and then

they were old enough for the married men, so easy
and fast and grateful—

no cleaning, no fights—just cars and the steep
slant of a summer night,

and the quick lie that an hour can be, the slickest one
after babysitting

his children, the road where they parked the one
with all the switchbacks—

deer dead in the ditches—and they took to it
like breaking into a house

just for the fun of it, like stealing someone
else's air, someone else's

darkness, the stuff even the smartest woman
will not miss. They were

her only wildness, and she would lie awake
for the hint of its return,

some man's smoke fast in its hair—
God's child dead asleep.

iwi

Her husband kept a small wooden kit filled
with buffing rags and brushes,

flat cans of polish with an image of something
like a bird on the lids.

Saturday evening meant taking it out
of the hall closet to polish

their good shoes for church, and that was where
she got the notion to do it—

fashion a canvas from a bedsheet or one
of his workshirts nearly

worn through. There, she would paint a translation
of what she saw reflected

in the kitchen window, her face the glass
she had to look through,

and what she could see of the world she saw
through it, indivisible

from the back pasture—her cheekbones, broomsedge
her hair, the tree line a widow's

peak, all of it she cast again and again
in what she had to—blacks

and tans, parade-gloss dew, oxblood lips. And when
she snapped the lid back on,

she could not help but consider the why
of the shy silhouette

of that bird, the two notes of its song unheard of
here, nothing left it

but the vestiges of wings—flightless, foreign—
and the familiar art of sorrow.

impossible bottle

what does a situation's sense of gravity do anything?

Impossible Bottle

❧

I recall it as a lens—thick, dimensioned—
its neck the stoppered

threshold to a chamber, the chamber
an encapsulation

of the ship, a clipper, graceful and lean, its sails
pristine, the delicate

threads of its rigging. That kind of green glass
my mother had seen

only on weather vanes or as decorative part
of a lightning rod, the glass's

survival sculpted proof of a strike that
had not yet happened.

❧

When I was small, we drove only one time
to the ocean, all of us

adds an odd sense of gravity

afraid of that kind of water, that horizon.
The day we left for home,

she told me to fill a bottle with air, to steal
some away as a souvenir

to open and breathe one winter night
when my attic bedroom

window would seal me in and threaten to let me
forget that day, its perilous air.

And she recalls exactly how the ship
got in there—suspended,

bottled against wind and water, driftless
in the dead sea of the cupboard

where she'd keep it; she was young then
and had never seen the ocean.

She was already wearing a ring on a chain
around her neck to hide it

from her mother. The ghost ship's arrival
was at the hands of a man

at the fair who took her money to let her
watch him slip the slim,

collapsed body into the bottle and then—
with a single practiced tug

of thread—raise it to the hereafter
of her house that is sealed

now as she says it must be for the very old.
She rarely opens a window,

even on the mildest day—impossible
as it has ever been

to worry too much about the wind.

phenomenal sensitivity here

is the wind mentioned elsewhere

My Mother Senses Them

Her mother preferred the Ouija for calling up
the dead, cajoling, cooing,

the talking-board set up on the kitchen table,
small portal in the planchette,

the letters it travelled forming words, a slow
slur. She says she hears,

no, senses them more easily than that,
the dead untranslated,

my brother closer than he was in life,
closer than when she

bore him, and his blue misery, into
this house—and his is

a nearness that does not frighten or forebode,
his arrival an owl's

coming up from the night-felled trees so silent
it is its own shadow,

or an astral body, and she does not
know whether it is

the walls or distance itself thinning—or
the world—to allow it.

my mother senses then too

The Outage

June thunderstorms, and a strike somewhere takes out
the house, the street, streetlights,

the whole of a small town darkened, its slippage
quick into a night

suddenly loud with after-rain, tree frogs,
cicadas, a whippoorwill—

with the way night thinks. A day, then two, the sun
rude as beauty, and still

she refuses to leave the house. She soaks
her feet in tap water,

drinks ice cream from her coffee cup, fanning
herself with the daily

devotion, the newspaper, her horoscope,
telling herself it is

what it is, the way she always has.
The television that

had been her distraction from the world
becomes vaguest mirror;

she leans into her flashlight's palsied beam.
The heat a haunting,

the silverware and china hot as though
from dishwater to the touch.

Is it for this—her sudden despair—
for what she cannot bear,

or that she cannot bear it?

Westerns

She chooses the known wild, tired now, the plots
formulaic, and she

knows them the way she knows her pound cake
and spoon bread, things she might

never make again but can recite—ingredients
and measurements exact

as the words of the apostles' creed she says
by herself on a Sunday morning.

And she prefers the ones in black and white
and shades of gray: dust,

tumbleweed, stampedes, rattlesnakes, some
savages, a drinking hole

now and again, the posse, a saloon's
swinging doors, the star

pinned to the chest of James Arness, who in life
and now in death refuses

to be old. The time will pass, and the sun
will set beneath the sill

of her kitchen window, her sink dry sometimes
for an entire day,

while every hour on the hour means the beginning
of another episode

she has already seen—the West not yet won,
thank God, and nothing settled.

The Earthquake

She thinks first not of the earth but of herself,
something happening

to her body alone, some sort of spell,
a seizure. But the frames

on the walls seize, too, the walls themselves
at a nervous pitch,

the floor's sudden cradling. The door breaks its lock
and swings open. She knows

it for what it is only when it stops, with shocked
clarity, the way

nothing alive ever has.

this is not about an earthquake

The Scar

The fainting she cannot recall—or the strike
of her face against

the table's edge—only the waking, the blood
in her eye from the brow-

bone, her mother's face so close to hers
she could not see her.

The remedy: to fill the gash with soot
from the stove—a quick

staunching, the firebox still hot with live coals.
The bleeding would stop,

and the wound heal over to this—palest
blue, reminiscent

of an eyelash tattooed, prettied as though meant,
something she might have

chosen for herself. She does not have to
tell it for me to see

a morning's shimmering heat, the rooms of that child's
house—her mother seeing her

the way she sees me through this indelible
sill of ash—

and behind it the fire that had given the stove-eye
its brightest-ever aura.